JAMES A. GARFIELD

His Life & Times

A Pictorial History

By

Richard L. McElroy

Daring Books

Canton • Ohio

Published by Daring Books,
Box 526G, Canton, Ohio 44701.

This book is available at special discounts for bulk pur-
chases for fund-raising, sales promotions, premiums, or
educational use. Special editions or book excerpts can also
be created to specification.

Library of Congress Cataloging-in-Publication Data

McElroy, Richard L., 1947-
James A. Garfield : his life & times.

Summary: A pictorial biography of the orator,
congressman, teacher, and Civil War General who became
the twentieth President of the United States.
1. Garfield, James A. (James Abram), 1831-1881--
Pictorial works. 2. Presidents--United States--
Pictorial works. [1. Garfield, James A. (James Abram),
1831-1881. 2. Presidents] I. Title.
E687.M47 1986   973.8 '4 '0924 [B] [92]   86-16584
ISBN 0-938936-51-4
ISBN 0-938936-45-X (pbk.)

Printed in the United States of America.

DEDICATION

This work is dedicated to the loving memory of three unique human beings: Dan McKelley, Tanzi Smith, and Joe Jones who, in their suffering and pain, reached out to others in need. Their faith, courage, care, and concern should serve as an example to us all.

ACKNOWLEDGEMENTS

After eleven years of research I have several people to thank, all of whom were most kind and considerate in helping me one way or another. First and foremost are Al Bixby of Columbus and Mark Weber of North Canton. Their skills in the art of photography saved me much time, effort, and expense. I wish to thank U.S. Congressman Ralph Regula and his aide Al Simpson, along with Mary Folger of Garrettsville, for assisting me in locating pictures and articles. Also, Paul Keller, Jim Eakin and Mary Miller of Canton and Ralph Iula and Jolene Limbacher of the *Akron Beacon Journal* provided me with a number of photographs. In addition, Laine Mull and Dale Irene Maugans at Lawnfield in Mentor, Ohio, and Carl Engel and Elroy Sanford of the Lake County Historical Society proved valuable in gathering and identifying old photographs. And a special debt of gratitude is owed to Tom Hayes of Canton, who helped give this work a needed touch of professionalism. Lastly, and most of all, I want to thank my family for their understanding and cooperation. The time spent away from my wife, Pamela, and our children, Matthew, Rachael, and Luke, cannot be made up, though I will try.

TABLE OF CONTENTS

PREFACE

This is not a biography. Two recent books, **Garfield**, by Allan Peskin, and **The Garfield Orbit**, by Margaret Leech and Harry J. Brown, are, in my opinion, the best works on the life of the twentieth President.

James Abram Garfield is the first United States President whose life can be documented through photographs. From his teenage years until his death in 1881, history has managed to capture his likeness on glass plates and film.

Inventor and painter Samuel F.B. Morse introduced photography to America when he returned from France in 1839. Soon the method of daguerreotype, named after Frenchman Louis Daguerre, became a popular sensation. By the middle and late 1840s, Americans were sitting still to be photographed.

This is the story of James A. Garfield in pictures. With this book we can witness the metamorphosis of the entire saga.

Garfield recognized the importance of photography, and as a U.S. Congressman, fought unceasingly to see to it that Mathew Brady was properly rewarded for his efforts in photographing the Civil War. After much opposition, Brady was finally given $20,000 by the government — a meager sum for a man who had spent all of his money and risked his life to document the War Between The States.

With these photographs we get a better look into America's past as well. Most of these pictures are surprisingly sharp and clear. This is a tribute to the early pioneers of photography. Look at the pictures, study the faces of the subjects, and try to envision these individuals as not just our ancestors, but people who altered the course of American history.

BIOGRAPHICAL SKETCH

The twentieth President of the United States came from the most humble of origins. Perhaps no other Chief Executive began life under such adverse conditions only to rise above his desolation, and achieve success to become the most powerful leader of his country. The story of James Abram Garfield typifies the ideal American who, through his own efforts, conquered the negative forces and influences to attain his goals.

Born in a log cabin on November 19, 1831, he was the youngest of five children. When Garfield was two years old his father died from complications incurred fighting a forest fire near their Orange, Ohio home. Mother Garfield and her family worked desperately to raise crops and keep the family together. Instilling in her children a sense of ambition, pride, and responsibility, Eliza Ballou Garfield also taught her youngest son the values of hard work and Christianity.

It became apparent that the red-haired adolescent Jim Garfield despised both farming and manual labor, in addition to a distaste for school. Imbued with a stubborn, adventurous spirit, Garfield left home at the age of 16 to work on the Ohio canal.

After nearly drowning three times, he contracted malaria before returning home (at the urging of his cousin Amos, on whose ore boat he had worked). Once again healthy, he found renewed interest in schooling. He attended Chester Seminary, then worked as a custodian and doing odd jobs so he could finish his education at the Western Reserve Eclectic Institute in Hiram, Ohio. There he learned the classics, the sciences, and developed a fondness for history. He also gained the reputation as a diligent student and an expert debater. Wanting to further his education even more, he went to Massachusetts to enroll at Williams College and graduated in 1856. He returned to the Hiram Institute and, just after a year, became president of that college.

Innovative and resourceful, he modernized the curriculum, and became an ordained minister with the Campbellites (Disciples of Christ). While preaching to various congregations in Ohio and parts of Pennsylvania and New York, he found the study of law intriguing. He was fascinated by politics as well, but found the conflict between religion and politics a dichotomy he would wrestle with the rest of his life. He soon discovered these two forces often dictated conflicting responses to public issues, and James A. Garfield could not always find a happy medium between the two.

In 1859, he was nominated for the Ohio Senate and was elected after campaigning on an anti-slavery platform. His service in the Ohio General Assembly was short-lived, however, when the southern states seceded from the Union. His pacifist ideals gave way to war. In 1861, he accepted a commission as a colonel and formed his own regiment — the 24th Ohio Volunteer Infantry.

Garfield saw action in Kentucky and Tennessee, serving under General Rosecrans and becoming a major general. Proving himself daring in battle and a good administrator, friends back home placed his name in nomination to the U.S. Congress. At the urging of President Lincoln, he resigned his position in the army to take his seat in the House of Representatives.

Garfield remained a Congressman for the next seventeen years. He joined the Radicals in Congress, supporting Negro suffrage and military occupation of the South. As a gifted orator and skilled politician, he eventually became a national figure and leader of the Republican Party. Through the influence of his friend and mentor Salmon P. Chase, former Secretary of the Treasury and Chief Justice of the Supreme Court, he learned the intricacies of government in the areas of economics and financing.

As a Congressman, Garfield made two important contributions in the areas of the Census Bureau and education. He modernized census methods and upgraded standards which have been in use more than one hundred years. Garfield was a strong supporter of education for all youths, advocating equal opportunity for minorities and the underprivileged. He was responsible for the creation of the National Department of Education, and saw to it that federal funds went to various colleges. To Garfield, education was not only a means of self-advancement — it was the salvation of our democracy. He felt if one grew up in ignorance, our nation would be headed toward disaster.

Regarded as a proponent of compromise on many issues, Garfield's legislative career was characterized by strong stands on "hard money" (currency backed by gold), reducing federal spending, cutting "red tape" and eliminating patronage and nepotism. Eventually he became chairman of the powerful Appropriations Committee, but by the mid 1870s, the Ohio Congressman found himself embroiled in a number of controversies. New York Senator Roscoe Conkling and other party bosses feared Garfield would destroy the spoils system. Their efforts to discredit him, however, failed. If this was not enough, Garfield was accused of accepting bribes from

corporations on at least three occasions. And though an avowed conservative on fiscal matters, he did little to endear himself to constituents when he voted for a congressional pay raise. Some answers to these allegations were never fully explained. Garfield's reputation emerged somewhat tainted, but each time he was re-elected to his 19th District seat.

Victory at the polls was overshadowed by poor health and personal problems. Because of his duties in Washington, he was constantly separated from his family. Two children died in youth, and Garfield was beset by periods of gloom and self-doubt. In 1876, a measure of tranquility came when the Garfields purchased a farm in Mentor, Ohio. Once settled in, they renovated and expanded the house. Today Garfield's home, Lawnfield, is a National Historic Site and open to the public.

Duty still beckoned, and as minority leader in the House, Garfield worked diligently to breach the differences between bickering factions within his own party. In 1880, he went to the Republican Convention in Chicago supporting Senator John Sherman for President, and opposed to Ulysses S. Grant gaining a third term. Grant's backers, the Stalwarts, challenged the Half Breeds, the new progressive wing whose candidate was the clever and pompous James G. Blaine of Maine.

Garfield nominated Sherman but the delegates remained deadlocked. As support for Sherman, Grant, and Blaine eroded, Garfield allowed his name to be put in nomination as a "dark horse" candidate. Finally, after 36 ballots, the gentleman from Ohio was chosen, with Chester Arthur

of New York as his running mate. Immediately the Republican nominee sought to heal party wounds. From his front porch in Mentor he conducted a successful campaign against Democratic opponent General Winfield Hancock. In an extremely close race, Garfield won by less than 10,000 votes from more than 9 million ballots cast. His electoral margin was only a bit more impressive. When he announced that Senator Blaine would be his Secretary of State, the Stalwarts screamed betrayal and promised revenge.

Garfield's "honeymoon" with Congress was short-lived. Refusing Roscoe Conkling's demands to appoint a Stalwart to the cabinet, the new Chief Executive asserted his authority to choose cabinet officers without Senate approval. His decisive and bold action against bossism gained for Garfield the support and respect of the public and simultaneously destroyed his political foes from New York. The President also convinced Congress to re-fund the national debt by offering public sale of government bonds. Efforts were underway to establish civil service reform, mend the wounds still existing between North and South, and reaffirm stronger ties between the United States and the nations of Latin America.

On July 2, 1881, Garfield prepared to leave Washington for a vacation. First, he would travel by train to pick up his wife, recovering from a bout of malaria at a seaside resort in Long Branch, New Jersey. Then, he planned to travel by yacht to New England, stopping at Williams College to enroll his two sons and receive an honorary degree. This would be followed by a visit with relatives and relaxing with his wife.

All of these plans, however, were cut short as Garfield, Secretary of State Blaine, and the President's two sons walked through a Washington depot. Charles Guiteau, a deranged office seeker who had been denied a post with the new administration, rushed up behind Garfield and fired two shots. One bullet grazed his sleeve, while the other lodged in his lower back. Doctors attempted to remove the .44 slug but their efforts failed. Soon his wound became infected, and over the course of several weeks Garfield grew steadily worse while losing nearly a hundred pounds. He sensed the end was near when he asked his friend, Almon Rockwell, "Do you think my name will have a place in human history?" Rockwell replied, "Yes, a grand one, but a grander place in human hearts."

James Abram Garfield died on September 19th, and an entire nation mourned. Within a few decades the memory of him seemed to fade. He became lost in the sea of Presidential faces between Lincoln and Theodore Roosevelt. As biographer Allan Peskin has so aptly described, ". . . Garfield would be remembered more for what he was than for what he did . . . [his] life tangled in contradictions . . . here was a misplaced intellectual thrown into the stage of public life, moving restlessly between the worlds of action and introspection, drawing strength from each but at home in neither."

GARFIELD QUOTATIONS

Few people, including historians, realize the many talents of James A. Garfield. He was, among other things, a farmer, canal worker, preacher, teacher, army general, philosopher, and politician.

Garfield also demonstrated his talents of writing. As a Congressman he would invite friends into his office, ask them to sit down, and recite a verse in English. With two pieces of paper and a pen in each hand, he would proceed to write the quote in Greek on one paper and Latin on the other, both at the same time. And if the size of a man's head is any indication of intelligence, Garfield had to have all of his hats specially made.

Perhaps the man, but not the name, has been forgotten. Thousands of streets, parks, and monuments throughout the country testify to his achievements.

This kindly gentleman from Ohio was an avid reader of the classics, and is recognized as a person of wit and wisdom. Within his letters and diaries, on pieces of scrap paper and congressional notes, he scribbled maxims concerning a wide range of topics.

Due to recent and renewed interest in Garfield memorabilia, most of these quotations have been preserved. Many of the following sayings came from letters and booklets discovered in the stacks of Garfield material at Lawnfield in Mentor. These quotes are profound, amusing, and even prophetic. Most have stood the test of time, and like those of Will Rogers, some remain astonishingly relevant in today's society.

ART —

True art is but the anti-type of nature — the embodiment of discovered beauty in utility.

We cannot study Nature profoundly without bringing ourselves into communion with the Spirit of Art, which pervades and fills the Universe.

CHANCE —

Nothing is more uncertain than the result of any one throw; few things more certain than the results of many throws.

Do not trust what lazy men call the spur of the occasion. Occasion may be the bugle call that summons an army to battle, but the bugle blast can never make soldiers or win victories.

Things don't turn up in this World until somebody turns them up.

If there be one thing upon this Earth that mankind love and admire better than another, it is a brave Man — it is a man who dares to look the Devil in the face and tell him he is a Devil.

EDUCATION —

Next in importance to freedom and justice is popular education, without which neither freedom nor justice can be permanently maintained.

If I were called upon today to point to that in my own state of which I am most proud . . . I would point to her common schools.

FAME —

As a giant tree absorbs all the elements of growth within its reach and leaves only a sickly vegetation in its shadow, so do towering great men absorb all the strength and glory of their surroundings and leave a dearth of greatness for a whole question.

A monopoly of popular honors is as much of a tyranny as a monopoly of wealth.

It has been fortunate that most of our greatest men have left no descendants to shine in the borrowed lustre of a great name.

FREEDOM —

Liberty can be safe only when suffrage is illuminated by education.

Unsettled questions have no pity for the repose of a nation.

Nations have perished only when their institutions have ceased to be serviceable to the human race.

It matters little what may be the forms of National Institutions if the life, freedom, and growth of society are secured.

There is scarcely a conceivable form of corruption or public wrong that does not at last present itself at the cashier's desk and demand money.

HEROES —

I love to believe that no heroic sacrifice is ever lost, that the characters of men are moulded and inspired by what their fathers have done; that, treasured up in American souls are all the unconscious influences of the great deeds of the Anglo-Saxon race, from Agincourt to Bunker Hill.

Eternity alone will reveal to the human race its debt of gratitude to the peerless and immortal name of Washington.

I doubt if any man equalled Samuel Adams in formulating and uttering the fierce, clear and inexorable logic of the Revolution.

Heroes did not make our liberties, they but reflected and illustrated them.

HISTORY —

After the battle of Arms comes the battle of History.

The lesson of History is rarely learned by the actors themselves.

History is but the unrolled scroll of Prophecy.

The developments of statistics are causing History to be rewritten.

All along the dim centuries are gleaming lamps which the mind has lighted, and these are revealing to Him (the historian) the path which Humanity has trod.

Battles are never the end of war; for the Dead must be buried and the cost of the Conflict must be paid.

Present Evils always seem greater than those that never come.

LAW —

Mankind has been slow to believe that order reigns in the universe, that the world is a Cosmos, not a chaos.

Coercion is the basis of every law in the universe — Human or Divine. A law is no law without coercion behind it.

We should enlist both the pride and the selfishness of the people on the side of good order and peace.

We legislate for the people of

the United States, not for the whole world; and it is our glory that the American laborer is more intelligent and better paid than his foreign competitor.

It is a safe and wise rule to follow in all legislation that whatever the people can do without legislation will be better done than by the intervention of the State and Nation.

POWER —

The possession of great power no doubt carries with it a contempt for mere external show.

LITERATURE —

Many books we can read in a railroad car and feel a harmony between the rushing of the train and the haste of the Author, but to enjoy standard works we need the quiet of a winter evening — an easy chair before a cheerful fire, and all the equanimity of spirits we can command.

He who would understand the real spirit of Literature should not select authors of any one period alone, but rather go to the fountainhead, and trace the little rill as it courses along down the ages, broadening and deepening into the great ocean of Thought which the Men of the present are exploring.

The true literary Man is no mere gleaner, following in the rear and gathering up the fragments of the world's thought; but he goes down deep into the heart of Humanity, watches its prophetic foresight, their tendencies, and thus, standing out far beyond his Age, holds up the picture of what it is and is to be.

I am in favor of passing a law that no author shall have a copyright of his book without having an index. It adds immensely to the value of a book and more than doubles its value to the reader. [Author's note: this book does not have one]

It is indeed an uninviting task to bubble up sentiment and elaborate thought in obedience to corporate laws, and not infrequently these Children of the Brain, when paraded before the proper authorities, show by their meagre proportions that they have not been nourished by the genial warmth of a willing heart.

MONEY AND FINANCE —

A government is an artificial giant, and the power that moves it is Money — money raised by taxation and distributed to the various parts of the body politic, according to the discretion of the Legislative power.

An uncertain and fluctuating standard is an evil whose magnitude is too vast for measurement.

Successful resumption will greatly aid in bringing into the murky sky of our politics, what the Signal Service people call "clearing weather."

The Gold Exchange and the Gold Clearing-House, of New York, will be remembered in history as the Germans remember the robber castles of the Rhine, whence brigand chiefs levied black-mail upon every passer-by.

SUCCESS —

You must not continue to be the employed. There is something, young man, which you can command — go out and find it and command it. If you are not too large for the place you are too small for it.

Behind every successful man sits a good lawyer.

Let not poverty stand as an obstacle in your way.

TRUTH —

There is a fellowship among the Virtues by which one great, generous passion stimulates another.

Truth is so related and correlated that no department of her realm is wholly isolated.

Truth is the food of the human Spirit which could not grow in its majestic proportions without clearer and more truthful views of God and his universe.

YOUTH

I feel a profounder reverence for a boy than for a man.

I never meet a ragged boy in the street without feeling that I may owe him a salute, for I know not what possibilities may be buttoned up under his coat.

MISCELLANEOUS

I have seen the sea lashed into fury and tossed into spray, and its grandeur moved the souls of the dullest men; but I remember that it is not the billows but the calm level of the sea from which all the heights and depths are measured.

No Man can make a speech alone. It is the great human power that strikes up from a thousand minds that acts upon him and makes the speech.

For the noblest Man that lives there still remains a Conflict.

The principles of Ethics have not changed by the lapse of years.

Growth is better than Permanence, and permanent growth is better than all.

All free governments are party governments.

It is cheaper to reduce crime than to build jails.

TIME LINE

1831 - November 19 James A. Garfield is born

1833 - father dies

1848 - August 16 worked on canal boat

1849 - March 6 attended classes at Geauga Seminary in Chester, Ohio
November 13 began teaching in one-room schoolhouse in Solon

1850 - March 4 "reborn" when baptized in the Chagrin River after joining the Disciples of Christ sect

1851 - March 19 taught school in Muskingum County
August 23 attended Western Reserve Eclectic Institute at Hiram

1852 - February 24 taught school in Warrensville

1853 - began preaching in area churches

1854 - July 11 entered Williams College in Williamstown, Massachusetts

1856 - graduated from Williams College

1857 - professor and president of Hiram College

1858 - November 11 married Lucretia Rudolph

1859 - October 11 elected to Ohio Senate

1860 - admitted to the Ohio Bar

1861 - August 21 commissioned Lieutenant Colonel of 42nd Regiment of Ohio Volunteer Infantry
November 27 promoted to Colonel
December 14 involved in battle at Big Sandy Valley, Kentucky

1862 - January 10 defeated Confederate forces at Paintville, Kentucky; promoted to Brigadier General
April 4 commanded brigade at Shiloh, Tennessee (saw limited action), developed camp fever
and given leave
September 2 nominated for Congress by district convention
October elected to U.S. House of Representatives from the 19th Congressional District

1863 - February appointed Chief of Staff under General Rosecrans
September took an active role in the battle of Chickamauga, Tennessee
December 1 daughter "Trot" dies
December 5 resigned from army at Lincoln's request to take his Congressional seat - served for
the next 17 years; chaired Banking and Currency Committee and Appropriation Committee

1867 - July 13 he and Crete sailed to Europe for a four-month tour

1876 - October 12 purchased farm in Mentor, Ohio
October 25 son Edward dies

1877 - member of the Electoral Commission which chose Hayes as 19th President

1880 - January 13 elected by Ohio General Assembly to the U.S. Senate
June 8 nominated for President by Republican Convention in Chicago
November 4 elected President of the U.S.
November 8 resigned U.S. House seat
December 23 declined Senate seat as President-Elect

1881 - March 4 inaugurated as President
July 2 shot by disappointed office seeker
September 19 died from wound while resting in Elberon, New Jersey

James and Lucretia Garfield had seven children, two of whom died at an early age, Eliza (Trot) at
age three in 1863, and Edward (Ned) almost two years old in 1876. Five other children growing to
adulthood were Harry, James, Mary (Mollie), Irvin, and Abram.

I

IN THE BEGINNING

James A. Garfield's roots in America were planted in Massachusetts. This is the home of Lieutenant Thomas Garfield, born December 12, 1680; died February 4, 1752. He was the third son of Captain Benjamin Garfield who lived in Watertown Township (later annexed to Concord then becoming the town of Lincoln, Massachusetts). Thomas built and occupied this house in Lincoln. His son, Thomas, Jr., also attained the rank of lieutenant in the local militia. Abram, the son of Thomas Jr., was in the fighting at Concord in April of 1775 where the "shot heard 'round the world" began the Revolutionary War. Not to be confused with the twentieth President's father, this Abram was a great uncle. In July of 1881, Garfield had planned to visit this old homestead, along with a stop at Williams College. An assassin's bullet, however, prevented him from making the trip.
(Credit Lake County Historical Society)

The X marks the site of the original log cabin near Orange, Ohio, in which Garfield was born. Garfield was only two years old when his father died, contracting pneumonia after fighting a forest fire near the home. Born November 19, 1831, the future President learned to work the farm along with his two older sisters and older brother, Thomas. The danger of Indians had vanished when the last Indian tribe, the Wyandots, left in 1820, but there were still the dangers of wild animals, deep ravines, and the hardship of human labor.
(Credit Lake County Historical Society)

Garfield's mother was born near Richmond, New Hampshire. This monument marks the location where her log cabin home once stood.
(Lake County Historical Society)

18

Perhaps due to his humble origins and the lack of material things others enjoyed, Garfield was very sensitive to criticism. He often dedicated himself to a given task with boundless energy just to prove to adversaries, both real and imagined, that he could master any work or responsibility. Pictured here is artist James Hope's conception of the birthplace of the "Last of the Log Cabin Presidents."
(Credit Lake County Historical Society)

This replica of the Garfield cabin now stands behind the grounds at Lake County History Center. Visitors may view the insides and tour the Garfield home from May through October.
(Photo by the author)

This photograph depicts the unveiling of a memorial on the site of the Garfield log cabin in Orange, Ohio, November 19, 1931 — the 100th anniversary of James A. Garfield's birth. James B. Garfield, a grandson, stands head up in the front row.
(Credit Lake County Historical Society)

The one-room schoolhouse in Orange County, Ohio, where Garfield learned the three r's.
(Credit Library of Congress)

In 1848, at the age of sixteen, Garfield worked aboard cousin Amos Letcher's ore boat, The Evening Star. Having nearly drowned several times, the youth became quite ill (probably malaria) and returned home. The accompanying early photograph shows a scene on the Ohio-Erie Canal.
(Credit Ohio Historical Society)

This sketch comes from an old woodcut in the Library of Congress, depicting Garfield as a boy working on the canal. This was an alternative for Garfield, for he preferred the open sea. At the port of Cleveland he was rejected by a "swearing and cursing" ship captain. Much of the time Garfield walked or rode mules or dray horses which pulled the barges. After his fourth trip from Cleveland to Pittsburgh, Garfield was promoted from driver to bowman, in charge of preparing the canal locks and doing other odd jobs. For this he received $14.00 a month, but by October he was making $20.00 monthly. Garfield also earned the respect of his fellow shipmates when he was challenged to a fight and won. By the end of October 1848, he was so ill, his fever did not break until the following January. In early March of 1849, Garfield's mother convinced him to attend school, using her entire savings of $17.00. Garfield later described himself at seventeen years old as "an overgrown, uncombed, unwashed boy..."

(Credit Akron Beacon Journal)

Much has been made of the fact that Garfield worked on the canals, but he remained only a short time. On one occasion, he fell off the boat only to be rescued by an alert boatsman who knew how to swim. Another close call came when he was accidentally knocked from the aft section, and a ship-mate threw him a lifeline. Pictured here is a canal boat in Ohio. Note the boy and horses on the right.
(Credit Ohio Historical Society)

In 1851, Garfield taught in a one-room Ohio schoolhouse similar to the one pictured here. He described the structure as dirty "as a black-smith's shop." One day a rowdy student larger than himself threw a block of wood and hit him in the head. After knocking the bully to the floor, the future President picked him up and threw him out of the building. The next day Garfield brought a bullwhip to enforce discipline, but his point was well made and he never had to use it.
(Credit Ohio Historical Society)

22

This is the Chester Seminary where Garfield attended school in 1849. It was here he met for the first time his future wife, Lucretia Rudolph. The Chester Seminary was actually a Baptist school, and Garfield was not altogether happy with its sectarian ways. Besides, he was a Campbellite (Disciple of Christ), and several months later he enrolled at the Western Reserve Eclectic Institute in Hiram.
(Credit Lake County Historical Society)

James A. Garfield as a teenager. This is probably the first photograph ever taken of the 20th President. The date of this portrait is about 1848. Better known for his wrestling and athletic prowess (as his father before him). the six-foot, red-haired youth began to think seriously of academics and religion.
(Credit Lake County Historical Society)

Taken in 1851 or 1852, this photograph shows Garfield (on the right) with his cousin and friend Henry Boynton. As a student at Hiram, Garfield often spent eighteen hours a day engrossed in his studies. He became a masterful debater and a top scholar.
(Credit Hiram College)

The Hiram faculty and families in the late summer of 1852. Only a few of the images can be identified. Number 3 is Mary Turner Hinsdale, 6 is Henry James, and 8 is Almeda Booth.
(Credit Hiram College)

A church in Poestenkill, New York where Garfield preached.
(Credit Lake County Historical Society)

Almeda Booth, a remarkable scholar and teacher at the Hiram Institute. She inspired Garfield to better himself, and he often credited her for his success. He cherished her friendship and looked upon her as almost a sister.
(Credit Hiram College)

The Garfields of Orange, Ohio. Left to right: James, Mary, mother Eliza Ballou Garfield, Thomas, and Mehitabel. Probably taken in 1852 or 1853.
(Credit Lake County Historical Society)

The Rudolph children, 1853. Left to right are Ellen (Nellie), John, Joseph, and "Crete." Ellen later married Camden O. Rockwell; Lucretia and James named their daughter after her.
(Credit Lake County Historical Society)

The Greek class at the Western Reserve Eclectic Institute at Hiram, April 1853. "Crete" Rudolph and Jim Garfield sit on the right in the front row. Just a short time before this photograph was taken, Garfield broke off his romance with Mary Hubbell of Warrensville. In time, however, he fell under the spell of Lucretia's charm and beauty. Lucretia's father, Zeb Rudolph, was a Campbellite and a trustee at the institute. Just a few moments before this photograph was taken, Garfield took the photographer aside and told him to arrange the subjects so Lucretia and Jim sat next to each other. (Credit Lake County Historical Society)

Mark Hopkins, president of Williams College and Garfield's favorite professor. Years later Garfield told friends his idea of education was Hopkins sitting on one end of a log and him on the other end. (Credit Library of Congress)

Garfield first sprouted whiskers as a senior at Williams College in 1856. This rare photograph shows a growth of several weeks. He sported a beard the rest of his life.
(Credit Lake County Historical Society)

For years the main building was the only educational structure at the Hiram Institute. Garfield outgrew the intellectual confines of the small college and sought further education in the east. Though he preferred Yale or Brown, he decided on a small school in western Massachusetts, Williams College.
(Credit Hiram College)

This is A.S. Hayden. In May of 1857 the trustees of Hiram Institute decided to replace Hayden as President. They chose an ambitious, determined twenty-six year old alumnus, James A. Garfield. At that time the faculty consisted of five teachers. Hayden's frequent absences and apparent lack of administrative responsibilities led to his downfall. Garfield, who also worked as a janitor at the institute, initiated reforms at Hiram, instituting science courses and supporting anti-slavery ideals. He also actively played chess. Such action created controversy among the college trustees and throughout the community.

(Credit Hiram College)

Early picture of Jim Garfield and Lucretia Rudolph. The lovely "Crete" had met her future husband years earlier at the Geauga school, then again at Hiram. They were married November 11, 1858 at the home of Zeb Rudolph in Hiram. The bride and her "attenders" wore "white dresses with low necks and short sleeves." A guest described the young ladies as a "galaxy of beauties." Ironically, Garfield married Lucretia due to a sense of obligation and duty. Though he had fallen in love with a couple other young ladies prior to his marriage, Garfield's love for his wife deepened in their years following matrimony.

(Credit Ohio Historical Society)

29

Lucretia's parents,
Arabella and Zeb Rudolph
(date unknown).
(Credit Hiram College)

The Hiram faculty in the spring of 1859. Garfield, as Principal and College President, is on the left. Lucretia is on the right end. As chairman of the faculty, Garfield earned $600 a year and taught six classes a day.
(Credit Hiram College)

Zeb Rudolph's home, built in 1853. It was here Crete and James were married. This photo was taken after an addition was built on the house.
(Credit Hiram College)

Garfield's home in Hiram: a winter scene.
(Credit Hiram College)

Garfield and his sister-in-law Ellen Rudolph. Taken in 1859, Ellen was four-teen years old.
(Credit Lake County Historical Society)

Arabella Rudolph, Gar-field's mother-in-law.
(Credit Lake County Historical Society)

An ambrotype of Garfield taken in 1859.
(Credit Ohio Historical Society)

II

THE GREAT REBELLION

Interior of Camp Chase, 1861. Conditions within the camps were horrible. Disease was rampant, discipline was non-existent (until 1862), and materials were scarce.
(Credit Ohio Historical Society)

An 1861 ambrotype of Camp Chase in Columbus. It was here that Colonel James A. Garfield had trained with his "Hiram boys" of the 42nd Ohio Volunteer Infantry. Having resigned his position as state senator, Garfield got sixty young men from the Hiram Institute to join the army. Just prior to his appointment, Governor Dennison had sent him on a secret mission to Illinois to procure supplies and weapons for Ohio's 30,000 volunteers.
(Credit Ohio Historical Society)

The war in Kentucky was one of constant drudgery and hardship. Torrential rains not only bogged down transportation but also took a heavy toll of casualties.
(Credit Ohio Historical Society)

Besides bad weather and sickness, Garfield's men faced enemy soldiers in the rough terrain of Kentucky and Tennessee. Losses for the 42nd O.V.I. were light, however. (Credit Ohio Historical Society)

A Mathew Brady photograph of one-star General James A. Garfield. Probably taken in 1863. Note the Napoleonic pose. (Credit Library of Congress)

The landing of Union men and supplies at Vicksburg, Mississippi in 1863.
(Credit Ohio Historical Society)

The battlefield at Missionary Ridge, Tennessee, looking from Orange Knob. Photo by George N. Bernard. Garfield saw heavy action within the area of Chattanooga.
(Credit Ohio Historical Society)

Ohio artillery unit, 1863.
(Credit Ohio Historical
Society)

General William S. Rosecrans and his staff. Rosecrans sits directly beneath the tree. His chief of staff, James A. Garfield, sits to Rosecrans' left, fifth man over from the right in the front row. Garfield and others complained of Rosecrans' incessant talking and indecision under pressure. Though he admired his commander, Garfield felt Rosecrans had made some blunders at the battle of Chickamauga. In a detailed report to Secretary of War Stanton and in conversation with Lincoln, Garfield both praised and criticized him. George Thomas, the "Rock of Chickamauga," later replaced Rosecrans as commander. This photograph was probably taken in Tennessee. (Credit Ohio Historical Society)

Garfield's pistol and sword, in a show case at Lawnfield, Garfield's home in Mentor. The revolver was stolen. Photo taken by Elroy Sanford. (Credit Lake County Historical Society)

General James Garfield and his staff. Sitting left to right are Henry Gist, Garfield, and Hunter Brook. Standing in back are Andrew Burt (left) and James Barrett. Photo taken in 1864.
(Credit Lake County Historical Society)

40

Garfield and many other noted personalities came to L.C. Handy's Studio in Washington, where Mathew Brady or an assistant captured their image on glass plate. Here, Garfield sits beside the famed Brady clock in 1863.
(Library of Congress)

Brady photograph of Brigadier General James Garfield. 1863.
(Credit Lake County Historical Society)

Probably taken in 1863.
Photographer unknown.
(Credit Lake County
Historical Society)

Eliza Arabella Garfield, nicknamed "Trot." Born on July 3, 1860, she died of diphtheria on December 1, 1863.
(Credit Lake County Historical Society)

Ohioan Clement L. Vallandigham, southern sympathizer and leader of the Peace Democrats or Copperheads. President Lincoln had him banished to the Confederacy. Garfield was in charge of delivering Vallandigham across the southern border. Vallandigham, however, found the Confederacy to his disliking and eventually fled to Canada, where he ran for governor of Ohio in absentia. Garfield warned the students at Hiram that if any of them identified with Vallandigham's cause, they would suffer harsh punishment.
(Credit Ohio Historical Society)

Secretary of the Treasury Salmon P. Chase. Chase became a close friend of Garfield's. When Garfield was summoned to Washington to give a report on the battle of Chickamauga, he was a guest of the Chases for a few weeks. During this time the young Brigadier General learned of Lincoln's cabinet meetings and the intricacies of Lincoln politics. Chase impressed upon Garfield the need for sound economic policies and a thorough understanding of finances.
(Credit Library of Congress)

It was rumored that Chase's daughter, Kate, and Garfield were lovers. Such gossip stemmed from Garfield's stay with the Chases in 1863. Crete became concerned about such talk until Garfield wrote her, poking fun at Kate's "pugged nose." This photo was taken shortly after the war when Kate was married to Senator Sprague of Rhode Island. It is unlikely that Garfield would betray both his wife and the friendship of Kate's father.
(Credit Ohio Historical Society)

Brady photograph of the two-star General, taken in 1864.

(Credit Library of Congress)

The 42nd Ohio Volunteer Infantry, mustered in on September 28, 1861. Many of the citizen-soldiers were "Hiram boys." Here is Company K encamped at Young's Point, Louisiana, in 1863. Garfield is not in the picture.
(Credit Gates Press of Cleveland)

President Abraham Lincoln convinced Garfield to resign from the army and assume his seat in Congress.
(Credit Library of Congress)

Civil War hospital, 1865. This one was located in the west side of Cleveland. (Credit Ohio Historical Society)

The Union Army on its way home. Here, a long line of supply wagons pass through Zanesville, Ohio in 1865. (Credit Ohio Historical Society)

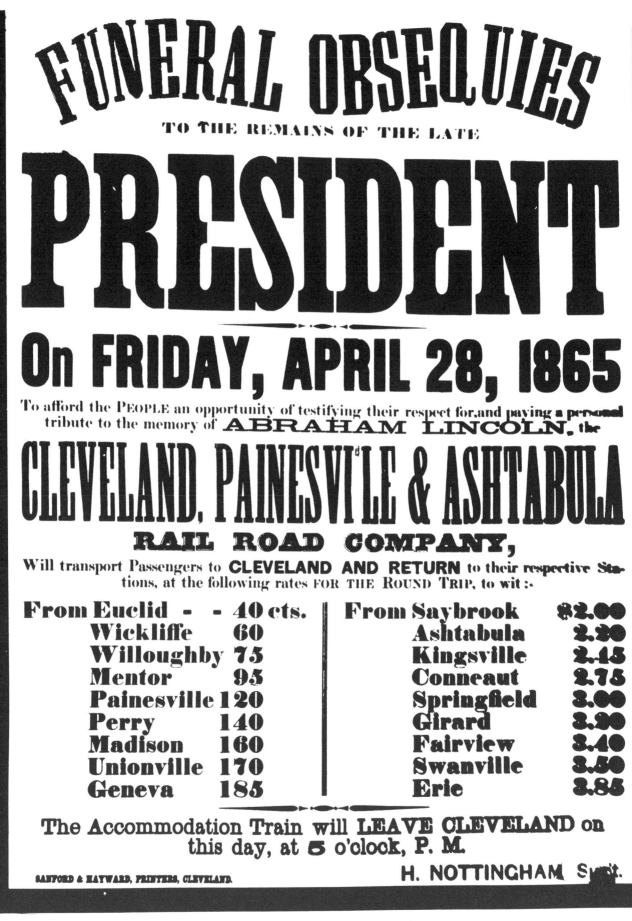

FUNERAL OBSEQUIES

TO THE REMAINS OF THE LATE

PRESIDENT

On FRIDAY, APRIL 28, 1865

To afford the PEOPLE an opportunity of testifying their respect for, and paying a personal tribute to the memory of ABRAHAM LINCOLN, the

CLEVELAND, PAINESVILLE & ASHTABULA

RAIL ROAD COMPANY,

Will transport Passengers to **CLEVELAND AND RETURN** to their respective Stations, at the following rates FOR THE ROUND TRIP, to wit :-

From Euclid	40 cts.	From Saybrook	$2.00
Wickliffe	60	Ashtabula	2.30
Willoughby	75	Kingsville	2.45
Mentor	95	Conneaut	2.75
Painesville	120	Springfield	3.00
Perry	140	Girard	3.30
Madison	160	Fairview	3.40
Unionville	170	Swanville	3.50
Geneva	185	Erie	3.85

The Accommodation Train will **LEAVE CLEVELAND** on this day, at **5** o'clock, P. M.

SANFORD & HAYWARD, PRINTERS, CLEVELAND.

H. NOTTINGHAM, Supt.

The railroad company offered special rates to view Lincoln's catafalque. This same company years later would bring people to Mentor, Ohio, where they could hear Presidential candidate James A. Garfield speak during his "front porch campaign." (Credit Lake County Historical Society)

Cleveland Public Square, 1865. Shown is the catafalque in which Lincoln was laid. At the time the Perry Monument stood at the intersection of Superior Avenue and Ontario Street. Garfield attended the memorial services.
(Credit Ohio Historical Society)

Clara Barton, friend of
James A. Garfield and
founder of the American
Red Cross. Garfield
worked with Barton in
getting the U.S. to become
a member of the Interna-
tional Red Cross.
(Credit Library of Congress)

50

III

NATIONAL POLITICS
AND A HOME

This photograph was probably taken during Garfield's first term in the U.S. House of Representatives.
(Credit Lake County Historical Society)

Long-bearded congressman in 1872.
(Credit Lake County Historical Society)

Garfield's Hiram home. Here he lived since his days as College President and Civil War officer. In 1869, he bought a house in Washington for $10,000, but still maintained this one. As an Ohio Congressman he also took an active interest in the old college, of which he was a trustee. In 1876, he and Crete bought the Dickey farm in Mentor, naming it "Lawnfield."
(Credit Hiram College)

Front porch of Garfield's former home in Hiram.
(Credit Hiram College)

A view from inside the
front entrance of Gar-
field's house in Hiram.
(Credit Hiram College)

Nellie Rockwell, Garfield's
sister-in-law. She is
holding her son, Arthur.
(Credit Hiram College)

The Garfield family and friends at the home of Zeb Rudolph in Hiram, 1873. Background left to right are Mother Garfield, James, Crete, Mrs. Joseph Rudolph, Irvin Garfield (the blurred figure), Carry Hill (neighbor girl, standing in the doorway), Joseph Rudolph, Zeb Rudolph, Mrs. Zeb Rudolph, Mary McGrath (nurse), and young Abram. The three children in the foreground are Harry A., James R., and Mary (Mollie) Garfield.
(Credit Ohio Historical Society)

The cradle in which all the Garfield children were raised.
(Photograph by Alford of Garrettsville, Ohio)

Garfield's mother in the early 1870s.
(Credit Hiram College)

56

Burke A. Hinsdale, Garfield's close friend. This picture was taken after the Civil War.
(Credit Hiram College)

Former Ohio Governor and the 19th U.S. President, Rutherford B. Hayes from Fremont, Ohio. Hayes, like Garfield, was a Civil War General and the two men were good friends. Hayes once advised Garfield that becoming governor of Ohio was "the surest road to the Presidency." This worked for Hayes, but Garfield chose to remain in Congress.
(Credit Ohio Historical Society)

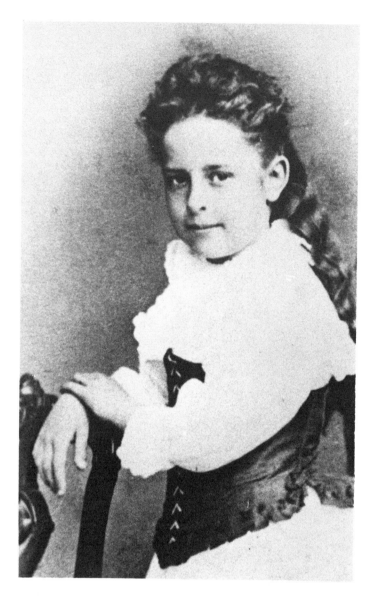

Painting of John Peter Robinson, done in 1880. Robinson was very helpful to Garfield during his congressional years, serving as advisor and financier. Also a close friend, Robinson made his money as a successful meatpacker in Cleveland.
(Credit Hiram College)

Portrait of daughter Mollie Garfield, later Mrs. Stanley-Brown. Taken in Washington by Julius Ulke in 1875.
(Credit Lake County Historical Society)

This photograph of Eddie Garfield, youngest child of Crete and James, was taken by Tosset in Washington. Born

December 26, 1874, Eddie died of whooping cough on October 25, 1876.
(Credit Lake County Historical Society)

Another picture of "Baby Eddie."
(Credit Lake County Historical Society)

58

"So my darling, you shall have a home and a cow," Garfield wrote Crete in 1876. As a U.S. Congressman he purchased this home and 150 acres from James Dickey of Mentor. Borrowing $18,000 on a five-year loan, Garfield completely renovated and added to the house. He dubbed it "Lawnfield," and today it is a state monument, open to the public from May through October each year.
(Credit Hiram College)

Rare full facial view of Garfield, taken by H.W. Tibbals of Painesville, Ohio. Date unknown.
(Credit Lake County Historical Society)

59

**James A. Garfield, prob-
ably in the late 1870s.
This photograph was
taken by Tipton of Get-
tysburg, Pennsylvania.**
(Credit Lake County
Historical Society)

This photograph of Garfield was taken by a Brady assistant and was discovered in the Brady National Portrait Gallery at 625 Pennsylvania Avenue in Washington, D.C.
(Credit Lake County Historical Society)

Engraved portrait of Garfield (source unknown). Probably taken from one of the county histories published in the late 1870s.
(Credit Lake County Historical Society)

This photo of Garfield and his daughter, Mollie, was one of Garfield's favorite pictures. Probably taken in 1875.
(Credit Library of Congress)

Garfield's living room at his house in Mentor.
(Credit Western Reserve Historical Society)

HOME OF JAMES A. GARFIELD.—MENTOR, OHIO.
THE LIVING ROOM.

Another picture of Eliza Ballou Garfield, taken in 1880 just after her son's nomination for President. Taken at Linwood Park in Cleveland.
(Credit Hiram College)

The Garfield family at Lawnfield, probably in 1880.
(Lake County Historical Society)

Mathew Brady, photographer. A friend of Garfield's, Brady was nearly blind when the U.S. Congress bought his Civil War photographs for $20,000. Congressman James A. Garfield convinced his fellow legislators that it was the least the country could do for a man who risked his fortune and life to take pictures. Garfield sought more than Brady received, believing the negatives and glass plates worth $150,000. The above picture was taken by a Brady assistant, Levi Handy.
(Credit Library of Congress)

Walt Whitman, photographed by Mathew Brady. James Garfield was a lover of poetry and the classics. Whitman was among his favorite writers. They had met on at least one occasion.
(credit Library of Congress)

IV

THE ROAD TO
THE WHITE HOUSE

In this photograph Garfield speaks at the 1880 Republican Convention in Chicago. Look closely and you can see him standing at the right. Garfield was chosen as a compromise, or dark horse candidate when delegates became deadlocked over the nomination of John Sherman, James G. Blaine, and U.S. Grant, who was seeking his third nomination to the Presidency after a four-year absence from the White House.
(Credit Ohio Historical Society)

On the day of his nomination at the Republican Convention in Chicago, Garfield stopped at 212 Wabash Avenue to have his picture taken at the Brand Studio.
(Credit Lake County Historical Society) 76

The Presidential campaign of 1880 was largely based on personalities, not issues. Buttons, posters, and campaign songs made the election a lively one. Propaganda, ignorance, indifference, and luck all played a role in putting James A. Garfield into the White House. He nosed out his opponent and friend, General Hancock, by a razor-thin margin of just under 10,000 votes.
(Credit Ohio Historical Society)

69

The Presidential candidate
in 1880.
(Library of Congress)

General Winfield Scott Hancock, Democratic nominee for President in 1880. This picture was taken prior to the convention; it was discovered later in a barn in upstate New York.
(Credit Library of Congress)

This photograph was taken shortly after Garfield's nomination in Chicago.
(Credit Ohio Historical Society)

Garfield's stand on civil rights and the Negro was inconsistent. This political cartoon, however, viewed the candidate as a Lincoln-like figure.
(Credit Library of Congress)

The Republican ticket of 1880.

(Lake County Historical Society)

The October 30, 1880 edition of Harper's Weekly shows a Thomas Nast caricature of Democratic nominee General Winfield Hancock being supported and controlled by the South, represented by an armed ex-Confederate slave holder.
(Lake County Historical Society)

THE REPUBLICAN PRESIDENTIAL CANDIDATE NOW ON VIEW.
CHARLES A. DANA:—"Come and see! Two cents a sight! Great Sun Microscope! Magnifies 100,000,000,000 Diameters."

Garfield's record is carefully examined in this 1880 cartoon. His stand on various issues is shown to the reader as somewhat tainted.
(Credit Ohio Historical Society)

FULL DRESS REHEARSAL OF THE GRAND PRESIDENTIAL CORPS DE BALLET.

An anti-Garfield cartoon, depicting the candidate as accepting a $329 payoff from the De Golyer Pavement Company of Chicago. He was also accused of taking bribes from several other corporations. Most of the accusations were never fully explained. In this photo, notice the De Golyer trap door and the number "329."
(Credit Ohio Historical Society)

Puck, July 14, 1880.

This is the front cover of Puck, July 14, 1880. Depicted here are Garfield and Hancock, demonstrating their respective (and similar) party stance on restricting Chinese immigration.
(Credit Library of Congress)

This group of black Civil War veterans came to hear Garfield speak in late September, 1880. Photo taken by J.F. Ryder of Cleveland.
(Credit Lake County Historical Society)

Joseph Keppler's cartoon of Garfield. It was entitled "From The Towpath to The White House."
(Credit Lake County Historical Society)

A Currier and Ives print entitled, "Backed To Win."
(Credit Library of Congress)

FARMER GARFIELD

Cutting a Swath to the White House.

Another view of Garfield.
(Credit Ohio Historical
Society)

Long Lane. This path led north from Lawnfield down to the railroad tracks. Thousands trekked an upward path for about three-quarters of a mile to enjoy a glass of lemonade and hear the candidate speak.
(Credit Lake County Historical Society) 89

Almost overnight Lawnfield became famous. Garfield decided to let the people visit him, instead of actively campaigning. Thousands came during the summer and fall of 1880. Although the Garfields were often inconvennienced, this new idea proved quite successful.

Special rates set up by the local railroad company brought eager crowds daily. In this photograph are some important figures. The four men standing next to the porch are Garfield, U.S. Grant, Roscoe Conkling, and Marshall Jewell, who became a member of Garfield's

cabinet. This visit was dubbed the "Treaty of Mentor" when disgruntled Republicans settled their differences. The visit by Grant and Conkling did tend to unify the party, but bad feelings still ran deep between bickering factions after the election.
(Credit Lake County Historical Society) 88

Election Day in Mentor, Ohio. Here local residents turn out to vote (for Garfield, of course) at the

Township Hall, located at the corner of Hopkins and Jackson Streets.
(Credit Lake County Historical Society)

Eliza Ballou Garfield dressed in her bonnet and black silk robe. With her bag packed for the inaugural ceremonies, Mother Garfield turned to her son and remarked, "Come James, we shall be left." Two hours later, the Garfield family boarded a train and left for Washington.

Eliza Garfield was the first mother to witness her son sworn in as President. Immediately following his oath, Garfield turned and kissed his mother, then his wife.
(Credit Lake County Historical Society)

A November 20, 1880
Harper's Weekly an-
nounces the victory. In
this cartoon Garfield rides
in a chariot, flanked by
Vice President-elect
Chester Arthur.
(Lake County Historical
Society)

Most northern newspapers were pro-Garfield. This front page political cartoon appeared in the New York Daily Graphic on

November 10, 1880. Garfield is depicted as trampling the four-headed Democratic beast.
(Lake County Historical Society)

81

1880 campaign banner
(private collection of Kenton Brovles).
(Credit Smithsonian
Institution)

In this political cartoon by
Joseph Keppler, U. S.
Grant concedes the 1880
Republican nomination
after being defeated in his
bid for a third term.
Roscoe Conkling and
other "Stalwarts" bow in
submission. From a June
16, 1880 edition of Puck,
this drawing was captioned
"The Appomattox of the
Third Termers — Uncon-
ditional Surrender."
(Credit Library of Congress)

"The Real Connecting
Link-This Looks Like
Business," was the caption
for this cartoon by
Thomas Nast which ap-
peared in Harper's Weekly
on March 26, 1881. It
celebrates the inauguration
of the 20th President by
having North and South
united by industry.
(Credit National Historical
Society)

Garfield's predecessor, Rutherford B. Hayes, was content to let Garfield resolve the problems of Civil Service. From a front cover of Puck, January 19, 1881. This cartoon was from the pen of Frederick Opper.

(Credit Library of Congress)

This carriage was used by Garfield in his ride to the Capitol for his inauguration. It was also used by his predecessor, Rutherford B. Hayes of Ohio, the 19th President.

(Credit Rutherford B. Hayes Memorial Library)

**Crete's inaugural gown,
now on display at the
Smithsonian.**
(Credit Library of Congress)

**Inaugural Ball invitations.
Tickets were available for
$5.00 and $6.00.**
(Credit Lake County
Historical Society)

Two inches of snow had fallen the night of March 3, 1881. A strong wind created drifts of two feet, and the parade looked doubtful. By 10:30 a.m. the next day, the sun had improved the sloppy conditions and General Sherman made final preparations for the parade. Troops from every state maneuvered into position under his command. As the Garfield caravan made its way from the Capitol to the White House, it passed under thirty-three iron arches, spanning the intersections of Penn-sylvania Avenue, and each one containing a coat of arms from the respective state. More than 100,000 citizens turned out for the festive occasion. In this rare photograph, troops march along Pennsylvania Avenue.
(Credit Lake County Historical Society)

Garfield delivers his inaugural speech before an estimated crowd of 17,000. The state of Ohio was well represented on this brisk March afternoon. Chief Justice Morrison Waite, Senators Pendleton and Sherman, former Presidents Grant and Hayes, Generals Sheridan and Sherman, Congressman (and future President) William McKinley, and Garfield's family made just a part of the proud group of "Buckeyes."

The new President's speech was well received. He stressed unity and compromise in healing the wounds which still existed between North and South. He promised more attention to farmers, manufacturers, and the national debt. He also rebuked the Mormon Church for practicing polygamy. Garfield ended his speech by denouncing the evils of nepotism and the spoils system, promising to restructure the civil service system. These last remarks created a stir in the crowd, as many had come to Washington hoping to find work on the government payroll. One of these individuals, a dim-witted office seeker who had contracted syphilis, would kill the 20th President.

Following a huge parade, Garfield and his family returned to the White House where his former college professor, Mark Hopkins, and 30 alumni from Williams College were entertained at dinner. The President and First Lady then attended the inaugural ball, held at the National Museum (Smithsonian) where guests paid six dollars for tickets. Shaking hands until his arm was sore, Garfield stayed until midnight. The next morning he awoke to the glorious burdens of his office.

(Credit Lake County Historical Society)

88

President Garfield's cabinet. Beginning at the top and moving clockwise are Thomas James of New York (Postmaster General), William Windom of Minnesota (Secretary of the Treasury), James G. Blaine of Maine (Secretary of State), William Hunt of Louisiana (Secretary of the Navy), Robert T. Lincoln of Illinois (Secretary of War), Wayne McVeagh of Pennsylvania (Attorney General), and Samuel J. Kirkwood of Iowa (Secretary of the Interior). (Credit Library of Congress)

This Currier and Ives print depicted Ulysses S. Grant being deprived a third term. Garfield's nomination and subsequent election dashed any hopes Grant had for another four years in the White House. Garfield and Grant had many political differences but among the traits they shared in common were a fierce patriotism, respect for the working class, and a fondness for cigars. Grant outlived Garfield by nearly four years, dying of throat cancer in 1885.

(Credit Library of Congress)

V

FROM TRIUMPH
TO TRAGEDY

Garfield's Inaugural ball at the opening of the new building of the National Museum (Smithsonian), from the sketch of an artist.
(Credit Library of Congress)

As an Ohio Congressman from Canton, William McKinley proved valuable to Garfield in the House. McKinley later served as Chairman of Garfield's Memorial Service in February of 1882. A Brady photograph.
(Credit Library of Congress)

BORROWED PLUMES — MR. JACKDAW CONKLING.

EAGLE. "Perhaps you would like to pluck me."

Garfield defeated the boss-controlled Senate in a dispute over Presidential appointing power. This victory was celebrated by Thomas Nast's cartoon of Senator Roscoe Conkling being "plucked" by a more powerful bird. This drawing appeared in Harper's Weekly on August 6, 1881.
(Lake County Historical Society)

Roscoe Conkling — the
brilliant, cold, eccentric,
and vain Senator from
New York. A powerful
boss, Conkling challenged
Garfield's powers and lost.

Garfield's assassin, Charles Guiteau, and hundreds of others treaded these White House steps to seek jobs and favors from the new President. Garfield never granted Guiteau an interview, but Blaine and others found him unsuitable for any responsible post. It was the aim of Garfield to create a civil service system whereby individuals were hired on merit by an independent agency. Nearly every President before Garfield complained of the burden and misery of interviewing countless office seekers.
(Credit Library of Congress)

Guiteau had twice followed Garfield in a feeble attempt to shoot him. Once, he even stalked the President to church, but lost his nerve during the worship service. Here the assassin strikes inside the Baltimore and Potomac Railroad depot as Garfield was departing for a vacation to New England on July 2, 1881. Accompanying the President were Robert Lincoln and James G. Blaine, his Secretary of State. One bullet passed through Garfield's coat sleeve, the other lodged in his lower back. The blood-stained tiles were later removed and given to the Smithsonian. After shooting Garfield, the assassin exclaimed, "I am a Stalwart. Arthur is now President of the United States." A moment later he surrendered to a police officer without resistance.
(Credit Library of Congress)

Garfield's sons, Hal and Jim, were with him when he was shot. Though he calmly told them the wound was not serious, he believed otherwise. Here, a messenger gallops from the White House gates through an anxious crowd just after Garfield had returned by ambulance.
(Credit Library of Congress)
106

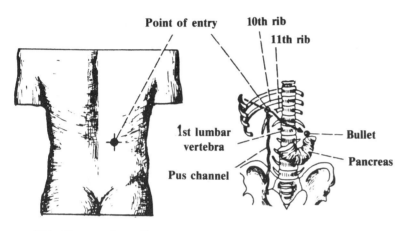

Point of entry

10th rib

11th rib

1st lumbar vertebra

Pus channel

Bullet

Pancreas

This diagram shows the bullet's point of entry into Garfield's back. In the skeletal drawing (frontal view) the bullet has passed on a downward angle, shattering the 11th, or floating, rib. It then passed through the first lumbar vertebra without damaging the spinal cord, lodging in muscle tissue near the pancreas.
(Credit Library of Congress)

In this Thomas Nast drawing, Lady Liberty sheds a tear for her fallen President. This sketch was published in Harper's Weekly on July 23, 1881.
(Credit Library of Congress)
107

ASSASSINS CELL—THE MORNING TOILET

The assassin in his cell.
Unbelievably, he received
many letters con-
gratulating him for
shooting the President.
(Credit Library of Congress)
109

The Washington, D.C.
railroad station where the
President was shot. Taken
from an early sketch.
(Credit Library of Congress)

Garfield's summer home in Long Branch, New Jersey.
(Credit National Historical Society)

Alexander Graham Bell was called in to try and locate the bullet which had perplexed the doctors.

Garfield was an admirer of Bell and envied the great inventor.
(Credit Smithsonian Institution)

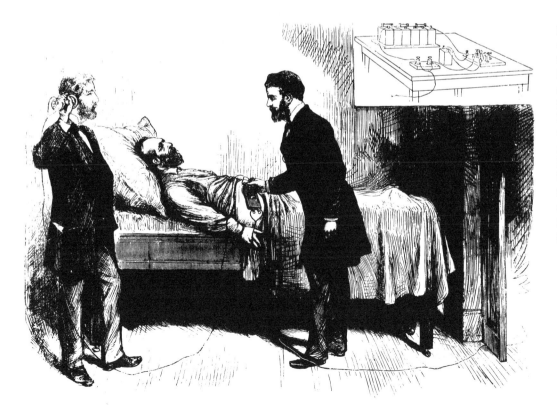

Doctors probed constantly with dirty instruments and their fingers to find the bullet. Garfield's physicians finally allowed Bell to try his "induction balance" method, which worked somewhat like a modern metal detector. Perhaps the steel springs in the bed interfered with the experiment. It failed, and the President died a month later.
(Credit Library of Congress)

Washington D.C
August 11ᴰ 1881

Dear Mother –

. Don't be disturbed by conflicting reports about my condition. It is true I am still weak, and on my back; but I am gaining every day, and need only time and patience to bring me through.

Give my love to all the relatives & friends, & especially to sisters Hitty and Mary – Your loving son – James A. Garfield

Mrs Eliza Garfield
Hiram, Ohio

A letter of hope and encouragement to mother. It was the last letter Garfield ever wrote.

(Lake County Historical Society)

99

WEEKLY NEWS.
EXTRA!

AMESBURY AND SALISBURY, MASS., SEPTEMBER 20, 1881.

DEATH

Claims our Beloved Ruler.

James Abram Garfield the 20th President of the United States of America,

Died Last Night at 10.34 o'clock.

The Heart whose Pulsations the World

Has so anxiously counted has ceased to beat.

A Pure, Upright and Successful Life

Laid down upon the Altar of his Country.

Death Sudden, though not Unexpected.

[By Telephone and Telegraph.]

FIRST DISPATCH.

Long Branch. N. J., Sept. 19, 1881.—10.34 o'clock P. M. The President is dead.

SECOND DISPATCH.

Long Branch, N. J., Sept. 20, 1881.—1.30 A. M.—At ten o'clock last night the President was apparently doing well and Attorney-General MacVeagh telegraphed to Minister Lowell that there was no expectation of an immediate change.

At 10.15 he called Dr. Bliss and complained of pains about the heart. At 10.34 he was dead.

Vice President Arthur was notified of the fact and asked to take the oath of office as early to-day as possible.

JAMES A. GARFIELD.

A Short Sketch of His Career.

JAMES ABRAM GARFIELD was born in Ohio, Nov. 19, 1831, making his present age within about two months of 50 years. His early youth was spent in alternate work and study. Ambitious but poor,he relied upon his own resources to obtain the education that has fitted him to grace the highest national position; in fact, the most elevated and honorable position on earth. He worked upon a farm, drove upon the towpath of the Ohio canal, and finally at about 20 he learned the carpenter's trade, which he worked at during vacation, while attending the Geauga seminary at Chester, Ohio. In 1851 he entered the Western Reserve College, at Hiram, Ohio, where in 1853-4 he was a student and teacher. In 1854 he entered Williams College, where he graduated with distinguished honor in 1856. He became classical teacher at Hiram, Ohio, of which he was elected the head one year later. Before entering college he had united with the Disciples' church, in which he had been brought up, and, according to the usage of that denomination, though never formally ordained to the ministry, he often preached. In 1858 he entered his name as a student with a law firm in Cleveland, though his study was carried on by himself at Hiram. Graduating from college in 1856, at the time of the organization of the Republican party, he cast his first vote that year for its candidate, and took active part in the campaign. In 1859 he was elected to represent the counties of Portage and Summit in the Ohio senate. He was an able public debater, and when secession broke out in 1861, he aided largely by his public speeches in moulding and shaping public sentiment and to make ready for national defence.

In August, 1861, he was appointed Lieut. Col. of Volunteers, and in September Colonel. In December he reported for duty to Gen. Buell, at Louisville, Ky., and was ordered, in command of a brigade of four regiments of infantry, to repel the rebels under Gen. Humphrey Marshall, from the valley of the Big Sandy River. He accomplished this task in Jan., 1862, defeating Marshall in the battle of Middle Creek, and forcing him to retreat from the State. He was commissioned Brigadier General, given command of the 20th Brigade, and ordered to join Gen. Buell. He reached with his brigade the battle field of Shiloh on the second day of the fight and aided in the final repulse of the enemy's rear guard. He participated in the siege of Corinth, and after its evacuation was detailed to rebuild the road to Decatur. In Oct., 1862, he served on a court of inquiry, and in Nov., on the court-martial which tried Gen. Fitz John Porter. In Feb., 1863, he joined the Army of the Cumberland, under Rosecrans, just after the victorious but severe battle of Stone River, and was appointed chief of staff. His success as a military man was rapid and brilliant. He rose to the rank of Major General by true merit.

Having been elected to Congress in 1863, he resigned his commission Dec. 3d, of the same year, and took his seat in the House of Representatives, where he served on the Military Committee until the close of the war. Jan. 24, 1864, he delivered a speech upon the confiscation of rebel property; Jan., 1865, upon the constitutional amendment abolishing slavery. In the same year he was assigned to the Committee on Ways and Means. In 1866 he made an elaborate speech on the public debt and specie payments. He also spoke in a masterly way upon the revision of the tariff. In fact, took leading positions on all matters of importance. His career in Congress was one which his constituency and the country regard with pride and satisfaction. One of the ablest thinkers and debaters, his voice of counsel was potent with his fellow-members, and counted largely in shaping the policy and destinies of the country to which his whole active life has been given, and in whose service he has laid down his life. With his more recent history the people are familiar. His honesty and sincere devotion to his political convictions, which to him meant the welfare of the fifty millions whom he represented, no one will question or doubt. He takes his place in history with the martyred Lincoln, and will hold as large a place in the loving memory of his countrymen as any who have preceded him.

In the Republican National Convention in Chicago, June, 1880, he was an earnest supporter of John Sherman for the Presidential candidacy. The contest was made between Gen. Grant and James G. Blaine; when, after more than thirty ballots, without a choice, the name of James A. Garfield was presented to the convention, all felt that the best man had come to the front, and he received the nomination. The result of the election showed the wisdom of their choice. The political ability displayed by him in his long and busy Congressional career, showing a rare familiarity with history; a refined literary culture, and warm magnetic power in oratory, has led him to be regarded by those most competent to pass upon his character, as a man possessing higher qualities of statesmanship and personal culture than any presidential candidate since Henry Clay. His literary culture has appeared in several articles which he has contributed to the various leading magazines and periodicals.

During the political campaign which resulted in his election, in the face of the bitterest assaults upon his character and record, he maintained that dignified silence which bespoke the nobleness and unselfishness of the man. His acts since his inauguration are before the world, and will stand the strictest scrutiny.

How prophetic the words spoken by him 20 years ago: "I regard my life as given to my country. I am only anxious to make as much of it as possible before the mortgage on it is foreclosed."

The tragedy which occurred on the 2d of July, showed how strong his hold was upon the American people. The country rose as one man, in condemnation of the villain's act, and a great wave of sympathy rolled in upon the capital from over the whole land. During the days, weeks and months which have passed while this death struggle has been going on, the world has stood with awe and reverence, listening with prayerful heart for tidings from the sick chamber, wherein lay the nation's chosen chief, the alternate hopes and fears which have beset the people, have at last culminated in the nation's loss of a pure and high minded statesman, in the death of one whose life has been a model one, and to whom history will accord a niche of fame in its loftiest temples.

Announcement of Garfield's death. He was the second President to die in office as a result of an assassin's bullet.
(Credit Lake County Historical Society)

A July 13, 1881 cover of
Puck depicting the crazed
assassin Charles Guiteau.
(Credit Library of Congress)

This sketch is from Frank Leslie's magazine, depicting the Franklyn Cottage where Garfield died. This 20-room summer home was located on the seashore. On September 5, 1881, more than 2000 volunteers worked to construct a 3200 foot track from the main line right to the door of this mansion. Guards were posted to insure privacy and quiet as the stricken President enjoyed the summer ocean breeze. "This is delightful....I am myself again," said Garfield. But his doctors had little hope that he could survive much more than a week. With the right side of his face paralyzed and sagging, his fever and pulse increased as more pus was drained from his wound and infected glands. Four days before his death he began coughing and vomiting, and experienced spasms and delirium. Garfield died at 10:35 p.m. on September 19, 1881 in this house.
(Credit Akron Beacon Journal)

**The assassin, Charles
Julius Guiteau, who was
executed in 1882.**
(Lake County Historical
Society)

A rare photograph showing the Executive Mansion in mourning, September 20, 1881.
(Credit Library of Congress)

The President's casket lies in state inside the rotunda of the Capitol.
(Credit Smithsonian Institution)

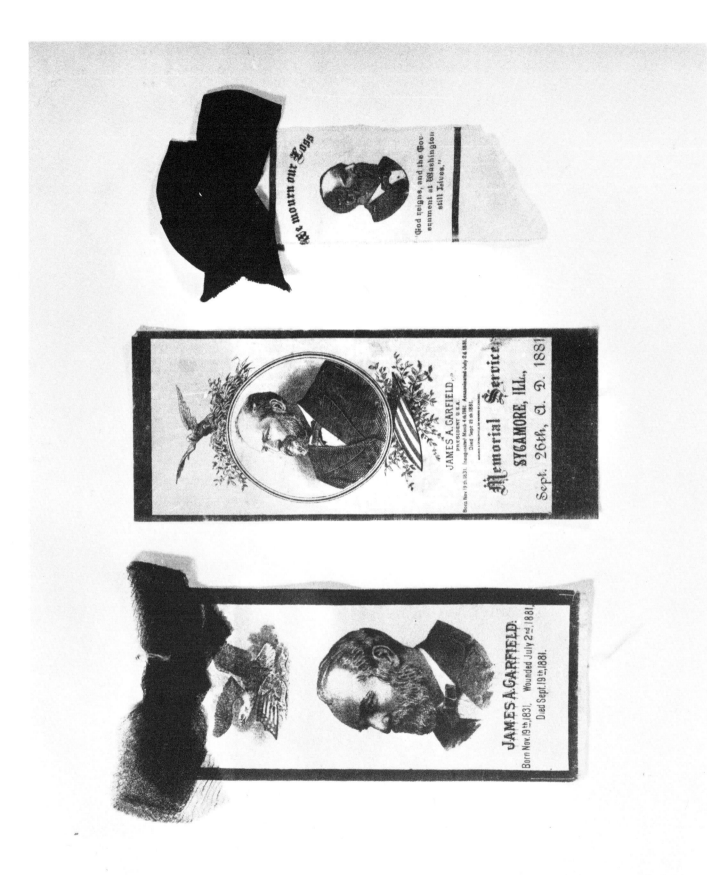

Memorial ribbons, bordered in black.
(Credit Smithsonian Institution)

The funeral train stops in Steubenville, Ohio, on its way to Cleveland. Notice Garfield's portrait at the front of the locomotive.
(Credit Lake County Historical Society)

Sheet music regarding Garfield's assassination (Ralph E. Becker collection).

(Credit Smithsonian Institution)

VI

REMEMBRANCE
AND A LEGACY

Garfield Obsequies in Cleveland. The miniature steamer "E.B. Nook" is draped in mourning. Notice the flags and portrait in black. Buildings in the background also have black bunting.
(Credit Lake County Historical Society)

Garfield Obsequies; view of the memorial pavilion
(Credit Lake County Historical Society)

Railroad tracks leading to the west arch.
(Credit Lake County Historical Society)

North section of the east arch, looking west. Inside is the funeral car, pavilion, and catafalque.

(Credit Lake County Historical Society)

An honor guard keeps watch over the President's casket during funeral services in Cleveland.
(Credit Lake County Historical Society)

Funeral choir, The German Singing Society of Cleveland. This photo was taken by C. Foljambe of 171 Superior Avenue.
(Library of Congress)

Balmoral Castle
Sept. 25, 1881

Dear Mrs. Garfield —

Though I have conveyed by telegraph the early profession of my true and deep sympathy with you in your terrible bereavement in this hour of overwhelming affliction, I am anxious to repeat these feelings in writing.

I have watched the long, and I fear at times, painful sufferings of your valiant husband and shared in the fluctuations between hope and fear the former of which decreased about two months ago, greatly to preponderate over the latter and above all I felt in deeply for you.

Sad experience has taught us but too well to dream what such always is to a devoted and loving wife — and that our Heavenly Father alone can give peace, resignation and strength to bear the heavy cross laid upon us.

That He may abundantly foresee your needs, only real assurance of comfort in this hour of deepest grief — is the prayer of yours

very sincerely,

Victoria R. I.

Pray convey to your children my sincere expression of condolence in their loss of such a Father.

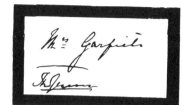

A letter to Crete from Queen Victoria.
(Credit Western Reserve Historical Society)

Lakeview Cemetery in Cleveland, September 26, 1881. The wording reads, "Lay Him to Sleep Whom We Have Learned to Trust, Lay Him to Sleep Whom We Have Learned to Love." Above the cross is a banner, "Come home to rest."
(Credit Lake County Historical Society)

The Honor Guard by the body of the slain President before entombment in the monument.
(Lake County Historical Society)

A memorial wreath.
(Credit Lake County
Historical Society)

**View of the bronze casket
in the receiving vault at
Lakeview Cemetery.**
(Credit Lake County
Historical Society)

**Marble carving by sculptor
C. Buberl, located above
the entrance to the Gar-
field tomb in Lakeview
Cemetery.**
(Credit Lake County
Historical Society)

**The remains of our 20th
President lie within this
memorial. Built at a cost
of $225,000 through na-
tional subscription, it was
formally dedicated on May
30, 1890. Located in
Lakeview Cemetery in
Cleveland, it is open daily
9:00 a.m. to 4:30 p.m.**
(Credit Lake County
Historical Society)

Invitation announcing official eulogy of the slain President. James G. Blaine, Garfield's Secretary of State whom he had defeated at the 1880 Republican convention, delivered the address. Senator John Sherman, who also lost the presidential nomination to Garfield, served as the Senate Chairman of the services. William McKinley, who would die from an assassin's bullet while President, was the House Chairman of this event.
(Credit Lake County Historical Society)

An aerial view of Garfield Monument.
(Credit Lake County Historical Society)

Domed ceiling of the Garfield Monument.
(Credit Lake County Historical Society)

GUITEAU TRIAL.

Pass _Mrs George Carter_

and _friends_ to Court Room this

day, December _1881._

God ≥ George Cockhill

during trial

No.

U. S. District Attorney, District of Columbia.

A pass to the assassin's trial. Though no doubt insane, Guiteau was hanged in 1882.
(Credit Smithsonian Institution)

Three photographs of Crete in the years following her husband's death.

Top left: (Credit Ohio Historical Society)

Top right: (Credit Rutherford B. Hayes Memorial Library)

Bottom right: (Credit Lake County Historical Society)

Front porch of the Garfield home in Mentor, taken in 1881 after the President's death. Left to right are James R., Abram, Crete, Mother Garfield, Thomas, Harry and Mollie.
(Credit Lake County Historical Society)

This picture of Thomas Garfield was taken by Crete. It was her brother-in-law's 87th birthday, October 16, 1909.
(Credit Lake County Historical Society)

Road sign in Poestenkill,
New York.
(Credit Lake County
Historical Society)

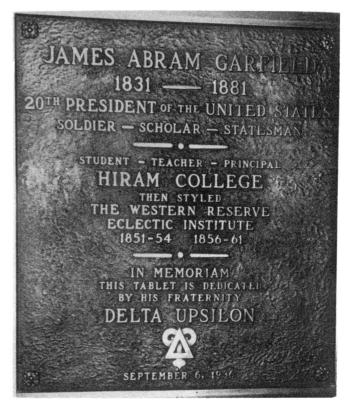

Memorial plaque on the
Hiram College campus. In
1867, the Western Reserve
Eclectic Institute officially
became Hiram College.
(Credit Hiram College)

**Mollie Garfield,
1867-1947. She married
Joseph Stanley-Brown,
press secretary to President James A. Garfield.**
(Lake County Historical
Society)

**The youngest son, Abram
Garfield, 1872-1958. A
graduate of Williams College and M.I.T., he was
an active member in the
American Institute of
Architects.**
(Lake County Historical
Society)

**Irvin McDowell Garfield,
1879-1951. Graduating
from Williams College and
Columbia Law School, he
became a corporate lawyer
in Boston.**
(Lake County Historical
Society)

**James Rudolph Garfield,
1865-1950. A graduate of
Williams College and Col-
umbia Law School, he
served in the Ohio Senate
(like his father), served on
the U.S. Civil Service
Commission, and became
Secretary of the Interior
under Theodore Roosevelt.
Photographer unknown.**
(Lake County Historical
Society)

Three of Garfield's grandsons who served in World War I. Left to right are James A. Garfield II (Harry's son), Rudolph Stanley-Brown (Mollie's son), and Newell Garfield (son of James R.). This picture was taken in 1917.
(Credit Western Reserve Historical Society)

This photograph of the Garfield family was taken 30 years after the President's death. Left to right are Irvin McDowell, Mollie, Abram, Lucretia, James Rudolph, and Harry Augustus.
(Credit Hiram College)

122

**Memorial plaque of the
twentieth President,
located on the front lawn
at the Garfield home in
Mentor.**
(Credit Lake County
Historical Society)

This statue of Garfield stands in front of the Capitol Building in Washington, D.C. where he served for 17 years in the U.S. House of Representatives before being chosen U.S. Senator and President. Erected by the veterans of the Army of The Potomac, it was unveiled in 1887.
(Credit Smithsonian Institution)

A bust of James A. Garfield in Statutory Hall of the U.S. Capitol.
(Credit Library of Congress)

NOTICE
KEEP OFF this
MOUND.

This monument was erected in the memory of President James A. Garfield at the Golden Gate State Park near San Francisco.
(Lake County Historical Society)

This is a Garfield display of memorabilia at the Akron-Summit County Library in April of 1981. The artifacts were borrowed from the archives at Hiram College.
(Credit Akron Beacon Journal)

A worker at Americraft, Columbus, uses a pneumatic chisel to put finishing touches on a new 2,716-lb. granite monument honoring Ohio's James A. Garfield (20th President of the U.S.). The memorial was donated to the city of Mentor by the Monument Builders of Ohio, a trade group of cemetery monument designers, stone sculptors and memorial builders.
(Credit Akron Beacon Journal)

HOME OF PRES. JAMES A. GARFIELD, MENTOR, OHIO — WEST VIEW OF MUSEUM

West view of Garfield's Mentor home, now a museum.
(Credit Western Reserve Historical Society)